ESSENTIAL **DK**

Strategic
Thinking

Andy Bruce
& Ken Langdon

DK

A Dorling Kindersley Book

Dorling DK Kindersley

LONDON, NEW YORK, SYDNEY, DELHI, PARIS
MUNICH & JOHANNESBURG

Senior Editor Adèle Hayward
Senior Designer Caroline Marklew
DTP Designer Jason Little
Production Controller Elizabeth
Cherry, Heather Hughes

Senior Managing Editor Stephanie Jackson
Managing Art Editor Nigel Duffield

Produced for Dorling Kindersley
by Cooling Brown
9-11 High Street, Hampton
Middlesex TW12 2SA

Design Arthur Brown
Editors Amanda Lebentz, Helen Ridge

First published in Great Britain in 2000 by
Dorling Kindersley Limited,
80 Strand, London WC2R 0RL

2 4 6 8 10 9 7 5 3

A CIP catalogue record for this book is available
from the British Library

ISBN-13: 978-0-7513-2798-4
ISBN-10: 0-7513-2798-0

Reproduced by Colourscan, Singapore
Printed in China by WKT Company Limited

See our complete catalogue at
www.dk.com

CONTENTS

ANALYZING YOUR POSITION

PLANNING A
STRATEGY

IMPLEMENTING
A STRATEGY

INTRODUCTION

The ability to plan long-term while maximizing performance in the short term is a must for managers. Strategic Thinking will help you to map out the route to success and build your analytical and team-planning skills. From researching and gathering the background information and arriving at a new strategy to reviewing and adapting it – all the key aspects of developing and implementing a strategy are clearly explained. There are 101 tips scattered throughout to give you further practical advice, while a self-assessment exercise allows you to evaluate your effectiveness as a strategic thinker. As you raise your ambitions to plan for the future, this will be an invaluable reference book to keep your thinking on course.

UNDERSTANDING STRATEGY

A strategy is a declaration of intent, defining where you want to be in the long-term. Understand the processes involved and how to avoid potential pitfalls to help you plan successful strategies.

DEFINING STRATEGY

Strategy was once defined as "the art of planning and directing large military movements and the operations of war". In business, a strategy maps out the future, setting out which products and services you will take to which markets – and how.

 1 Understand why a strategy is important for you and your business.

 **2** If you are unsure of the strategy of your organization, ask your superior to clarify it for you.

WHY HAVE A STRATEGY?

Having a strategy enables you to ensure that day-to-day decisions fit in with the long-term interests of an organization. Without a strategy, decisions made today could have a negative impact on future results. A strategy also encourages everyone to work together to achieve common aims. Most organizations have a strategic plan at the highest level, but some do not communicate it all the way down. A strategy is equally important whether you serve external customers (those outside your organization) or internal customers (those in departments or sections within your company).

LOOKING TO THE FUTURE

Today's business environment puts pressure on people to complete urgent tasks, meet day-to-day objectives, and overcome short-term problems. This is operational, or short-term, planning – and it often tends to take precedence over planning for the future. Strategy concerns itself with what is ahead, looking at where you are going, and how to get there. Even if you already know which products and services you are taking to which markets, you will still need a strategy to make it happen.

FOLLOWING THE STRATEGIC FRAMEWORK

Analyze information to understand your position

Pinpoint your competitive advantage

Define the scope of your products and markets

Decide where you want to focus your resources

Identify, prioritize, and implement change

Continuously monitor performance and review strategy

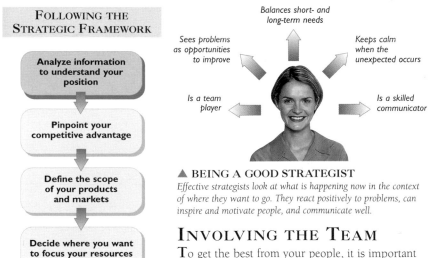

Balances short- and long-term needs

Sees problems as opportunities to improve

Keeps calm when the unexpected occurs

Is a team player

Is a skilled communicator

▲ BEING A GOOD STRATEGIST

Effective strategists look at what is happening now in the context of where they want to go. They react positively to problems, can inspire and motivate people, and communicate well.

INVOLVING THE TEAM

To get the best from your people, it is important to work within a clear framework that clarifies how they will be expected to help you to develop and then implement a strategic plan. Think of the methods and processes involved as a "map" that the team can follow to achieve success. By creating such a framework, you encourage the team to pull together and work to a common goal. You also promote their personal development by teaching them to think strategically.

EXAMINING THE PROCESS

There are three distinct phases to developing a new strategy: analysis, planning, and implementation. It is vital to devote time and effort to the first two stages, but also to maintain momentum throughout implementation to ensure ultimate success.

3 Involve everyone on the team in gathering information.

4 Encourage people to look objectively at the facts.

ANALYZING THOROUGHLY

During the analysis phase, you will collect as much background information as you can to help you make informed decisions. This stage is crucial because the facts you have to hand will influence the direction you decide to take. You will analyze what is happening inside your organization, looking carefully at aspects of your own and other parts of the company that may influence the plan. You will also find out what your customers want, how your competitors operate, and what the research trends or developments in your industry are. Your aim is to draw up a clear statement of the strengths and weaknesses of your position as well as a list of opportunities for the future.

DELEGATING RESEARCH ▼

Assign fact-finding exercises to members of your team. Information can be gleaned from publications, the Internet, and from talking to customers and contacts.

Manager provides research guidelines

Team member researches the competition by monitoring rival Web sites

PLANNING STRATEGY

Having gathered all the necessary facts, the next phase is to make strategic decisions that will bring you closer to your overall aim. You will need to take into account where you have advantages over the competition and establish the boundaries within which you will operate. The first step will be to list the products and services likely to be in demand in the future, and the markets that are available to you. You will then choose which of these markets you wish to develop, whether with existing products and services or new ones. Similarly, you will choose which markets it would be beneficial to leave. The decisions you reach will help you to establish your future financial position and work out a realistic budget.

5 Set aside ample time now to avoid rushing the planning stage.

6 Be prepared to listen to your team – every step of the way.

QUESTIONS TO ASK YOURSELF

Q Can I outline the strategic process to others?

Q Do I know where to look for the information I require?

Q Am I prepared to put enough time into the first two phases of developing a new strategy?

Q Can I get the support of my superior in establishing a new strategy?

BUILDING A STRATEGY ▼
There are three stages in the strategic process: analysis provides the basis for making choices, planning provides direction, and implementation brings the results.

IMPLEMENTING STRATEGY

During the final phase of developing a strategy you will determine, on the basis of your analysis, what you are going to do and how you are going to do it. It may be possible to achieve your aims with little change to the way the team works. On the other hand, you may find that success depends upon making far-reaching changes and learning new skills. Do not make the mistake of working so hard on the analysis phase that planning and implementation receive less overall effort – this will result in less effective strategies and incomplete implementation. You will also need to communicate the strategy to everyone who needs to know about it, and adapt it to take on board any changes in circumstances and in the activities of the rest of the organization.

Analyze → **Plan** → **Implement**

THINKING SHORT- AND LONG-TERM

The ability to differentiate between short- and long-term thinking and strike a balance between the two is an integral part of strategy. Understand the importance of both in strategic planning and you will find it easier to achieve the right combination.

7 Be confident about the future but realistic about what you can achieve.

8 Work hard for long-term goals while striving for immediate results.

KNOWING THE PITFALLS

Short-term planning deals with the here and now, or a few weeks hence, while long-term thinking takes you far into the future. If you focus entirely on short-term success, you risk long-term failure. For example, you may find yourself selling out-of-date products or targeting markets whose requirements have changed. If you place undue emphasis on long-term planning, today's business will inevitably suffer. The key is to focus on the present to achieve the growth you need now, and to keep one eye on the future to ensure that good decisions today are just as beneficial tomorrow.

◀ LOOKING AT THE LONG TERM
Sometimes the delivery of a quick sale is not in the best long-term interests of the business. Although this may mean that you face a difficult time with your customer in the short term, you are more likely to give them maximum satisfaction in the long term.

CASE STUDY

Elizabeth worked for a company that sold automated warehouse equipment. One of her customers was experiencing problems caused by a lack of capacity on a moving belt. Elizabeth wished to sell her customer two new belts to rectify the situation. However, when she placed an order for the belts with her production department, she was told that there was a new strategy to replace the old belts with new, superior, higher-tech products in about nine months' time. She informed her customer of this fact and also worked out a temporary solution to alleviate his problem. Although Elizabeth did not receive an order for short-term delivery, she did offer a much better solution to her customer, which resulted in a larger order at a later date, as well as the customer's continued goodwill and assured long-term business.

9 Make the effort to build strategic thinking into your everyday life.

ACHIEVING BALANCE

Striking the right balance between short- and long-term thinking takes effort and discipline. If you cancel a strategy meeting, it will have no short-term impact, but if you fail to return a customer's call, you could lose an order. It is hardly surprising, then, that unless a team is determined to give time to strategic issues, short-term operational tasks will always take priority. Allocate the appropriate time and resources to operations and strategy and stick to that plan. For example, you might decide to set aside three months to develop a new strategy, allocating two days of meetings to get started, and one day a week thereafter. That still leaves plenty of time for dealing with operational issues.

◀ **WORKING OUT A TIMETABLE**
By working out a timetable for producing and maintaining your strategic plan, you are committed to focusing on the long term. Keep to that timetable and avoid being distracted by operational issues.

WORKING STRATEGICALLY

Strategy is a continuous process; even when your plan becomes operational, you cannot neglect future planning. Set aside one day each month to discuss maintaining and developing the plan with the team. The most successful business people allow at least half a day per week to implement the strategic part of their jobs. They talk to customers regularly and review the roles of their team. Do a little work often on the plan to keep it fresh and ensure that team members stay committed and focused.

10 When making day-to-day decisions, consider the long-term implications before committing to action.

PREPARING FOR STRATEGIC SUCCESS

An effective strategic plan has accurate information, strong ideas, and committed people at its core. Involve the right people from the outset, then encourage them to research facts, and brainstorm for ideas to achieve the best possible plan.

11 Make every step in the planning process practical and achievable.

QUESTIONS TO ASK YOURSELF

Q Will this person add to the quality of the plan?

Q Do I need his/her commitment to implement the plan fully and successfully?

Q Does the plan require people with specific knowledge and/or expertise?

Q Will this person work well with the rest of the team?

INVOLVING KEY PEOPLE

An effective team is essential for a successful strategy. Involve the whole team early on in the planning so that they feel part of the process. Managers sometimes avoid team planning at this stage because they are not sure that all the people involved will play a significant role in implementing the strategy at a later date. Yet team planning is always useful: it allows you to assess team members as well as giving them the chance to decide if they are happy to work within the new strategy as it develops, or whether they feel they could make a greater contribution in another environment. Your core team should comprise all those people responsible for implementing the plan and achieving its aims.

◀ **ASSESSING TEAMS**
Involving key team members in strategy planning from the outset enables you to assess whether they have the qualities necessary to help you implement the plan in the future.

INVOLVING OTHERS

IDENTIFYING KEY STAKEHOLDERS ▼

Many people may be interested in the new strategy, but it pays to involve only those who will make the biggest contribution. Make sure you invite key stakeholders to the appropriate planning meetings.

People with an interest in or an influence on the new strategy are known as "stakeholders". Foster good relations with them, since they often provide experience or information, or can help with the analysis and decision-making. Strategic planning often requires people from different areas of the organization, such as sales and production staff, to formulate a plan together. This spirit of co-operation invariably produces the best results. The more involved key people feel in the process, the more likely they are to support the output and help during the implementation phase. Beware of involving too many people, however, as this may slow down the whole process. Too large a team is also likely to operate like a committee where finding an agreed decision becomes more important than finding the right one.

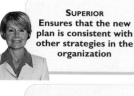

SUPERIOR
Ensures that the new plan is consistent with other strategies in the organization

EXPERT
Provides specialist knowledge of issues or opportunities that may affect the plan

BACKER
Lends support to the strategic plan by providing resources or budgets

KEY CUSTOMER/SUPPLIER
Provides valuable information on future requirements and new possibilities

TEAM
Relies on support from stakeholders inside and outside the organization

12 Change the make-up of the team if you feel you need to strengthen it.

GAINING COMMITMENT

Once you have developed your strategy, it is vital that the team does not start to lose interest during implementation. It is your role as manager to ensure that everyone understands the importance of the long-term strategy and is dedicated to making it happen. First, everyone should agree that a new strategy is needed. Second, everyone involved in the strategic process must feel confident that, guided by their manager, they have developed the right plan. Third, everyone must feel personally committed to making the strategy happen. Make the team aware that operational pressures are not an excuse for missing target dates involved in implementing the strategy.

 13 Make sure team members remain committed to achieving the plan.

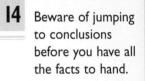 **14** Beware of jumping to conclusions before you have all the facts to hand.

POINTS TO REMEMBER

- A positive, motivational atmosphere can be created by involving everyone and being open to suggestions.
- Your own commitment to the strategy can be used as an example for others.
- The team should be encouraged to check the facts.
- Brainstorming begins at the beginning and never stops throughout the strategic process.

GETTING THE RIGHT FACTS

The importance of basing your strategy on the right information cannot be stressed enough. Poor data may lead to a crisis when the correct facts come to light, meaning the whole plan may need to be changed. The same goes for using out-of-date facts or for failing to collect all the information. Bear in mind that a poor strategic plan can lead to long-term failure and disappointing short-term results. At some stage, you will have to stop gathering facts in order to move on, even if you do not have everything you need. Resolve that at a later date.

AVOIDING GUESSWORK

Successful strategies must have strong factual foundations. Relying on guesswork or estimates could lead to a strategy collapsing, so avoid these at all costs, no matter how convincing they appear. Get all the relevant information before reaching a conclusion. Where there is a lack of data, look at the range of options on which you will base decisions once the information becomes known.

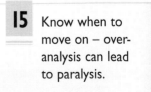 **15** Know when to move on – over-analysis can lead to paralysis.

BRAINSTORMING IDEAS

Coming up with ideas is paramount in strategic planning, whether it is thinking of key trends to be monitored, pinpointing possible product choices that could be made, or suggesting new and innovative ways to gain a competitive advantage. Throughout the strategic process, you and your team should meet regularly to brainstorm ideas. Write down a number of ideas in no particular order on, say, a flipchart, refine them, and then sort them into groups. The finished list will become part of the plan, although it will take several sessions to create the final strategic plan.

16 Give everybody at a meeting the chance to air their views in turn.

▼ ENCOURAGING CREATIVITY

To get the most from a brainstorming session, create a comfortable, relaxed environment where everyone feels free to express ideas. Seating should be kept informal, with no desks.

Each team member takes a turn to record ideas on a flipchart

Team leader expresses opinions but does not dominate the debate

Team member feels encouraged to be spontaneous

Team member listens and contributes without taking notes

LOOKING TO THE FUTURE

*C*ontinuous strategic thinking in a changing world is vital if you and your business are to maintain a winning position. Anticipate change rather than simply react to it, and adapt your strategy as necessary to keep moving ahead.

17 Remember that the planning process never comes to an end.

18 Adjust plans as circumstances change – radically, if necessary.

REVIEWING DECISIONS

Your strategy must be reviewed on a regular basis; the market does not stand still and neither do your competitors. A product or service that a customer has found interesting and satisfying over a long period of time may not be viewed so favourably in the future. Whole organizations have been caught out because a product feature introduced by a competitor has been taken up by the consumer and become desirable, even fashionable. It is very important to be ready to embrace such changes in the market and react quickly and positively if you failed to anticipate them in the first place. But, above all, aim to be the proactive person who first brings out a new feature, not the person who simply reacts to it.

AVOIDING STRATEGIC DRIFT ▼

This diagram illustrates how, by anticipating change in the external environment, the proactive team manages to give customers what they want before they even ask for it. The reactive team, on the other hand, is always one step behind.

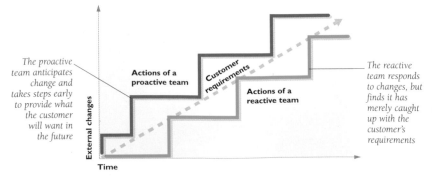

The proactive team anticipates change and takes steps early to provide what the customer will want in the future

Actions of a proactive team

Customer requirements

Actions of a reactive team

The reactive team responds to changes, but finds it has merely caught up with the customer's requirements

External changes

Time

▲ DETERMINING CUSTOMERS' NEEDS
Meet with customers periodically to find out what they expect from you, and carry out extensive market research on a regular basis to help you to anticipate their future needs.

AVOIDING PITFALLS

The best teams strive to be leading players rather than followers. Teams operating without a strategic plan find themselves constantly trying to gain lost ground. For example, customers may complain that a product lacks a desirable feature, so you put through a special order to get as near as you can to their request. Then your premium service is offered as standard by a competitor. Consequently, you lower prices or spend money to improve the service, but you still remain one step behind your customers' expectations. Their criteria for buying have changed from what they were when you devised your strategic plan initially.

19	Think the unthinkable; you can make it happen.

20	Never assume that you know what people think; always ask them.

STAYING AHEAD

To succeed in the future, it is necessary to put time and effort now into predicting what your customers will want and then guide the market towards adopting your customers' view of the future. Use the information your team gathers from sales and support staff, who have direct customer contact, to get a step ahead, and then work to maintain that lead. The most effective teams use innovation to stay in front of the market and the competition; take the example of the forward-looking garage that negotiated with a bank to install a cash machine on its forecourt long before any of its competitors.

ANALYZING YOUR POSITION

A strong strategy is derived from an analysis of your business. Assess environmental influences, customers, competition, and internal capabilities before forming your strategic plan.

EXAMINING INFLUENCES

There are many factors that may affect your performance. Study the economy, technology, and any legal and political changes related to your organization to identify new product and market trends that could influence your strategic planning.

21 Use analysis to lead you to strong conclusions and good decisions.

QUESTIONS TO ASK YOURSELF

Q How strong is our local currency, and will that affect our export business?

Q Does our organization take a strong line on environmental issues? If so, what does that mean for this team?

Q Are fuel prices expected to rise in the future, possibly because of tax increases, thereby reducing profits?

LOOKING AT THE ECONOMY

Most strategies depend to some extent on what is happening in the local and global economy. Look for issues that may have a radical impact first. For example, if you anticipate that interest rates will go up in the next six months and then stabilize, this may determine how and when you spend money on developing new products. Alternatively, if you sell products to or provide a service for tourists, you will want to know the best predictions for the growth of tourism in your area. Make a note of that trend and use the information when working out budgets.

EXAMINING TRENDS IN TECHNOLOGY

The dramatic pace of technological change has had an enormous impact on most organizations. The merging of communications techniques with computer information is steadily changing the way we all have to work. Guard against any dangers or problems that new technology may introduce by discussing the latest relevant technological developments at your planning meetings. If necessary, consult an expert or familiarize yourself with analysts' reports. Ask someone on the team to read the appropriate journals and give brief but concise updates to colleagues on a regular basis.

ASKING "SO WHAT?"

In analyzing your position, you will create a huge pool of data, some of it irrelevant to your strategic plan. Make the information more manageable and appropriate by subjecting it to the "So what?" question. If the answer is "So nothing", then that information has no impact on the strategy. Disregard it and move on.

22 Read widely to keep up to date with new trends and ideas.

UNDERSTANDING LEGAL AND POLITICAL CHANGES

As an increasing number of organizations, particularly in the public sector, find themselves operating within regulatory frameworks, it is vital to understand exactly what the rules are. If you are part of a government organization, you may have to take into account a change in the political party of the executive. In any case, you are subject to current employment laws which may have an impact on your strategic plan. Internal policy documents may need to be made available to the team, or you may need to ask a legal adviser to help you with your fact-gathering. Again, if you are not sure what data you need, brainstorm the possibilities with the team.

Employment lawyer advises on redundancy legislation

◄ **TALKING TO EXPERTS**
If you need information about the effect that certain legal or political changes may have upon your strategic plan, ask an expert in that field for advice.

UNDERSTANDING YOUR CUSTOMERS

The driving force behind any plan is what the customer wants from you as a supplier. Analyze why your customers buy from you and what their ideal is, then prioritize their needs to ensure that you design your strategy to serve them better.

23 Look at the service you provide from your customers' point of view.

24 Appoint a team member to discuss your organization's performance with customers.

IDENTIFYING BUYING CRITERIA

Customers trade product or service features against the price they are willing to pay for them. They also judge the quality of their relationship with a company's representatives and whether business processes give them customer satisfaction. To build customer loyalty, understand their buying criteria. What questions will they use to compare you with your competitors? Ask people in your organization who deal directly with customers for their input, and take into account potential customers as well as existing ones.

DEFINING THE IDEAL

Find out what your customers see as the ideal offering in four main areas: product, process, people, and price. Ask for their opinion either in a meeting, on the telephone, or by inviting them to be present at part of the planning session. An internal customer, for example, will tell you why he or she might turn to an external supplier to replace your service. These points make up the buying criteria and will fit into one of the four factors mentioned above.

POINTS TO REMEMBER

- Not all customers have the same desires and expectations.
- If customers are asked the right questions, they are more likely to tell you exactly what they want.
- Achieving a customer's ideal may be impossible, but knowing what it is will help you to come close.
- New or potential customers should not be overlooked.

PRIORITIZING CRITERIA

Having identified your customers' buying criteria, the next step is to decide which are the most important to them. The priorities you set now will have an impact on the decisions you make later in the planning process regarding your products, processes, people, and prices. Think about the relative importance of the criteria to each other when it comes to deciding on which changes to make to improve your service; you do not want to work hard on issues that the customer thinks less significant, particularly if that means putting less effort into issues they believe to be vital. If the team finds it difficult to agree on priorities in any of these areas, go back to your key customers again for their views and, if necessary, make good use of the brainstorming technique to discuss the possibilities.

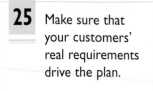

25 Make sure that your customers' real requirements drive the plan.

▼ **SETTING PRIORITIES**
Work out customers' priorities by listing their criteria in four key areas: product (what you supply); process (how you deal with customers); people (the quality of those who deal with customers); and price (cost to the customer). Note what customers would ideally want against each one. Finally, prioritize the criteria by rating how important the ideal is to the customer on a scale of 1–10. The higher the figure the greater the priority.

A first-class product is listed as an important criterion

Supplying a product that is simple to use is given highest priority

Ensuring that one person can respond to all queries is rated as a lower priority

	Criteria	Customer Ideal	Priority
PRODUCT	Quality	Zero faults	7
	Ease of use	No special training required	10
PROCESS	Ease of ordering	Fast and efficient order systems and delivery	8
	Administration	Accurate invoices and statements	6
PEOPLE	Knowledge of their product and services	One person able to answer all questions	3
	Customer knowledge	Able to relate products to customer's needs	4
PRICE	Competitive	Lowest price available	7
	Payment terms	Favourable credit terms to allow spread payments	6

ANALYZING COMPETITORS

Understanding your customers and meeting their expectations will only result in success if your performance exceeds that of the competition. Analyze your competitors' capabilities to identify potential opportunities and threats.

26 Learn from your competitors' failures as well as their successes.

27 Use competitive analysis to build team spirit.

FOCUSING ON ANALYSIS ▼

Remember that at this stage you are not making decisions. Do not take action, even if you spot an opportunity, until you move into the planning process. Then use your findings to make the right strategic choices.

EXAMINING COMPETITORS

If you have many competitors, choose a few key ones to analyze. Obtain competitors' brochures and promotional material to ascertain what they see as their strengths and how they present them to customers, and look at trade journals for product comparisons and reviews. Customers can be a source of competitive knowledge, as can new recruits who have come from a competitor. Make a chart of your competitors' ability to meet your customers' criteria, so you can see where they are nearer to the customers' ideal than you are.

Team member looks over competitors' brochures

Leader controls meeting to prevent rash decisions

Colleague highlights weakness in a rival organization

Team member notes opportunity and resolves to exploit it in the plan later

CULTURAL DIFFERENCES

North Americans tend to have a quicker and more widespread acceptance of new technology opportunities than Europeans; this can give them a competitive advantage over their rivals in Europe. It also means that if you are marketing a new technology in Europe, the North American market cannot be used as a benchmark for its success.

ENVISAGING THE FUTURE

Most organizations see their current competitors as providers of similar products or services. But in the future this may not be the case. There is often more than one way of doing things. If, for example, you run a helicopter service ferrying people out to an exclusive conference centre, a current competitor may be another contractor offering to run the same route. But future competitors might be video-conferencing companies who would render the journey completely unnecessary. Think about what your customers' requirements are likely to be in the future and research additional ways of meeting their needs. Bear in mind that your competitors are certain to be doing this too.

ASSESSING OPPORTUNITIES

Once you have completed your competitive analysis, you will be able to see clearly where there are major differences between your capability to meet your customers' priority criteria and your competitors' ability to do the same. Where you are significantly nearer to meeting your customers' ideal than your competitors, you will probably find that later on in the planning process you will have an opportunity to exploit this fact and, by so doing, to sell more products and services.

28 Keep information on the behaviour of competitors – it may come in useful later.

29 Never ignore a threat but build a way of dealing with it into the plan.

IDENTIFYING THREATS

Where your approach and abilities are similar, the customer will see no particular advantage in buying from you or your competitor. Where the competitor has a significant advantage, you may choose to reduce this threat to your success when it comes to making decisions later. Think widely about the possibilities, because other organizations will be doing the same when considering their prospects in terms of your customers.

ASSESSING YOUR SKILLS AND CAPABILITIES

Analysis of processes, information systems, resources, and team skills enables you to plan within your capabilities. However, rather than allow weaknesses to limit strategy, note areas for improvement and aim to build them into the plan later.

30 Remember that no business process lasts for ever.

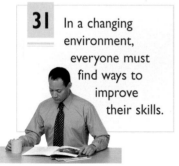

31 In a changing environment, everyone must find ways to improve their skills.

EXAMINING INTERNAL BUSINESS PROCESSES

Your business processes must be efficient if you are to impress customers. Examine them all closely and note those that need working on. You may need to review the way you take and confirm orders, revise terms and conditions, change how you inform staff of an order and distribute your products, and reassess the after-sales service you provide. Look particularly for duplication, gaps, and frequent areas of complaint.

ACCESSING INFORMATION

Examine how well your information systems, whether computerized or manual, provide people with the right information in the right format at the right time. Ask members of the team to note instances when their work has been delayed because they have had to spend precious time chasing information that could have been included in an easily accessible standard report or document. You may need to brainstorm to draw up a comprehensive list of information gaps. Finally, decide which of these gaps prevents the team giving a first-class service to its customers.

QUESTIONS TO ASK YOURSELF

Q Can I easily find the answers to customers' questions if I do not already know them?

Q Do I have to regularly correct information I receive?

Q Do I ever have to ask someone to wait because a certain piece of information has not yet reached me?

Q Am I always aware of how close my results actually are to my targets?

REVIEWING TEAM SKILLS

Ask people to talk about their strengths and weaknesses in relation to meeting customer needs. Try to make them feel positive about the process; after all, you are discussing formulating a new strategy that will bring the team greater success and more opportunities in the future. Review resources so you can be sure that nothing is preventing you from giving first-class service to the customer. Look at office accommodation, factory space, and warehousing, and assess how well they meet your needs now, and how suitable they will be in the future. Similarly, think about machinery, vehicles, and computer equipment.

▼ **PUTTING THE TEAM AT EASE**
When assessing the team's strengths and weaknesses in an open meeting, make sure everyone feels at ease. Use positive body language such as direct eye-contact.

EXAMINING INTERNAL CAPABILITIES

Review internal business processes

↓

Examine information systems

↓

Evaluate facilities and equipment

↓

Assess the skills and experience of the team

↓

Agree internal capabilities

↓

Note areas for improvement

DISCUSSING STRENGTHS AND WEAKNESSES

While some people feel secure enough to speak about their strengths and weaknesses openly, many do not. Start by discussing everyone's strengths, and it will then be easier to talk about areas for improvement, particularly if you use positive questions such as the following:

❝ *How has your job changed since you started work here?* ❞

❝ *How, broadly, could we all improve our performance?* ❞

❝ *Do we offer enough training?* ❞

❝ *Are there times when you find yourself in a difficult situation and are uncertain of how to tackle it?* ❞

SUMMARIZING THE ANALYSIS

Analysis produces a wealth of information. It is important to extract the most valuable elements, or those that will have the greatest effect on your strategy, and document them in a summary. Use this as the starting point for the planning process.

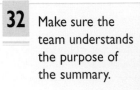

32 Make sure the team understands the purpose of the summary.

33 Use a quick SWOT analysis to solve any problems as they arise.

CREATING A SWOT SUMMARY

Bring the mass of information you have collected during the analysis phase into a manageable summary using a SWOT matrix. SWOT is an acronym for Strengths, Weaknesses, Opportunities, and Threats. You have already listed external trends, studied your customers and competitors, and reviewed your internal capabilities. Now pick the key elements and group them under the SWOT headings. The SWOT summary is a structured exercise that helps to clarify the team's views, acts as a powerful "driver" of the plan, and provides a way of measuring progress.

ASSESSING YOUR SWOT ▼

A SWOT summary details your strengths, weaknesses, opportunities, and threats, often in the form of a matrix. The chart below highlights questions you can ask to help you decide which key elements from your analysis belong under which headings.

UNDERSTANDING YOUR TEAM'S SWOT

STRENGTHS
What is the team competent at? What is the team really good at?

WEAKNESSES
Where is the team short of resources or capabilities? Where does it have competitive disadvantages?

OPPORTUNITIES
How could the team boost its sales to customers and improve its service? Where are there new markets?

THREATS
How might your products and services be overtaken? Which markets are deteriorating?

CULTURAL DIFFERENCES

Business people in Asia tend to fear "losing face" if they admit to deficiencies, so they tend not to list so many weaknesses. The British concentrate too much on their weaknesses, overlooking their strengths. The French have a reputation for original thinking during SWOT brainstormings.

DOCUMENTING FINDINGS

When compiling your summary, make sure that the strengths you have identified are truly of benefit to the customer. For example, if the customer wants a fast response to problems and you have set up a software-based help desk, then that is a strength. If you have highly skilled staff but no help desk, that is a weakness. By listing your weaknesses, you will be able to identify key areas where you could improve performance and service (which you document as opportunities). List as threats those issues in your analysis that, if ignored, may damage your ability to succeed.

SHARING THE SUMMARY

Before you use the summary as a basis for your strategic plan, show it to your stakeholders. This allows them to point out any areas of misunderstanding or issues that are already being addressed elsewhere in the organization. It may also be useful to share your summary with key customers. You may choose to remove any sensitive information from the summary before showing it to them, but remember that most relationships benefit from openness. When you eventually produce the strategic plan, the summary will give you a number of drivers. Look for ways in which you can use your strengths, remove your weaknesses, exploit your opportunities, and avoid or overcome threats. Since you have spent time analyzing what is important to the customer, you can be confident that your final plan will be "customer driven".

QUESTIONS TO ASK YOURSELF

Q Is it easy to see the main drivers of my business by looking at the SWOT summary?

Q Is the language used in the SWOT summary clear, concise, and simple?

Q Have I validated the summary with enough stakeholders by discussing it with them?

Q Does the entire team agree to all the points in the summary?

▼ REVIEWING THE SWOT SUMMARY

Use the SWOT summary as a tool to determine the underlying assumptions of your strategic plan. Remember that it needs to be reviewed regularly and kept up to date for it to be effective.

| Use the SWOT summary as basis for strategy | → | Review every three months | → | Amend SWOT to reflect the current situation |

PLANNING A STRATEGY

An effective strategic plan is developed methodically, drawing on the in-depth analysis that has been carried out. Now is the time to make a series of choices that will form the basis for change.

STAGING THE PROCESS

A strategic plan is formulated in stages, involving the team and any stakeholders you may wish to include. The decisions you make at each step will give your strategy direction, while a final test will check that the focus is right prior to implementation.

 34 Always consider the implications of a decision before finalizing it.

35 Enlist the help of others to make the plan as successful as possible.

SETTING OUT THE STAGES

The first stage in building a strategy is to define your aims. Once you have a clear direction, you will be able to determine where your competitive advantage lies, or what your team or organization has that is unique and that customers want. You will then need to set boundaries and choose areas on which you wish to focus, decide which stakeholders you wish to consult as you go through the process, and work out a time-scale. As a guideline, a simple plan can probably be worked out within a couple of days, while a complex one could take up to three months.

PLANNING STRATEGY IN STAGES

STAGES	FACTORS TO CONSIDER
DEFINE PURPOSE Create a definitive statement of future goals, agreed with superiors, team members, and stakeholders.	● Your purpose must fit in with the strategic aims of other departments and teams in the organization. ● The statement should be kept brief and clear, concentrating on simple definitions of intent.
DETERMINE ADVANTAGE Compose a brief statement identifying why customers will buy from you rather than anyone else.	● Other stakeholders, such as the marketing team, may help in deciding on your competitive advantage. ● The advantages must be enduring, since strategy focuses on the long term.
SET BOUNDARIES List the products and markets you will deal in and those you definitely will not, approved by the entire team.	● Too many boundaries will make the team inflexible; too few will prevent the team from focusing clearly. ● If team members have pet schemes for products or services, they should air them when setting boundaries.
CHOOSE AREAS OF EMPHASIS Identify products and markets that are considered worthwhile areas for more time and resources.	● Dividing products, services, markets, and customers into groups will help with choosing priorities. ● Emphasis will need to be reviewed on a regular basis as circumstances change.
ESTIMATE A BUDGET Examine the costs of allocating resources to product markets and forecast expected profits.	● In organizations with a standard budgeting process, an expert in this field should be involved. ● Other stakeholders may be needed to supply information for cost estimates.

36 Never assume you have everything right. Review and update your decisions regularly.

CHECKING THE STRATEGY

At the end of the strategic planning process, you will list the key criteria of the new strategy in a template, known as a "business case template". This is used to test both current activities and future ideas, or business scenarios, to ascertain whether or not they will fit in with your strategy. If, for example, a criteria is to keep service staff to a minimum, an idea for new, high-maintenance product would fail to measure up against the template. You could either discard the idea, or make it fit the template by altering the product or service, or putting more resources into that market.

DEFINING YOUR PURPOSE

E very business must have a primary purpose. Why do you and your team exist in your own organization and in the context of the outside world? Define your aims and agree on a statement of purpose to keep you focused as you develop the plan.

 37 Make sure that your team is able to state its purpose.

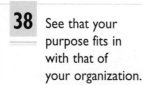 **38** See that your purpose fits in with that of your organization.

CONSIDERING AIMS

If your superior has asked you to start the strategic planning process, you may be given a definite set of aims at the outset. If you are creating the strategy for yourself, then define your aims by discussing them with others. Think about the wording you use, since your purpose forms the first boundary for the strategic plan and should help all stakeholders understand where the strategy will lead.

INVOLVING OTHERS IN DEFINING PURPOSE

MANAGER
As manager, you have overall responsibility for deciding on your team's purpose, but it is important to discuss your aims with colleagues throughout the organization, and outside it if necessary, in order to agree on the direction to take.

SUPERIORS
Talk to superiors about your aims, since they will have to check that your strategic purpose fits in with that of the organization overall.

STAKEHOLDERS
Involve stakeholders to help draft your aims and refine the wording. They may have valuable suggestions to make on getting the focus right.

TEAM MEMBERS
Ask key members of the team to agree the final definition of aims, taking into account any suggestions made by superiors and stakeholders.

39 Talk through your aims with other teams to foster good relations.

DISCUSSING AIMS WITH COLLEAGUES

Teams fit within organizations and, to operate effectively, need good links with other teams. Make sure that your team understands how its strategy fits in with those of other teams within the organization, and appreciates the aims of cross-functional teams with whom it has dealings. Some organizations have a formal structure in place for communicating strategic aims among staff, but if one does not exist, it is up to you to ensure that your team's aims are made known.

CREATING A PURPOSE STATEMENT

Ask your team to come up with a simple definition of what it is going to sell to what markets. Do not be tempted to write a "mission statement" because these tend to be long and rather vague. Instead, make sure that the team concentrates on creating a statement that is succinct and clear, based on the good research it has carried out on customers and competitors.

40 Keep your statements of purpose short, to the point, and action-orientated.

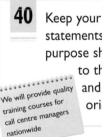

We will provide quality training courses for call centre managers nationwide

STRENGTHENING PURPOSE STATEMENTS

WEAK STATEMENTS	QUESTIONS RAISED	STRONG STATEMENTS
"We will concentrate on exploiting our considerable experience in food products."	Will you only be selling products? Where do you intend selling them?	"We will supply food products and services to North American markets (mainly Canada) in the first two years of our overseas operation."
"We will become the centre of excellence for the company in information technology."	Who and where are your customers? What do you think you will be doing for them?	"We will provide computer hardware, software, and application systems to all the departments in head office."

DETERMINING COMPETITIVE ADVANTAGES

*Your distinctive capabilities, or whatever
your team or organization does that sets
it apart, form the backbone of your strategy.
Carefully review your analysis in order to
create a statement that clearly sums up
your enduring competitive advantages.*

41 Remember that
whoever won
yesterday may not
win tomorrow.

STARTING A REVIEW

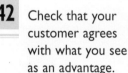

42 Check that your
customer agrees
with what you see
as an advantage.

To pinpoint your enduring advantage, first
review your findings from the initial three analysis
stages. Look at the trends identified in your
analysis of the environment to see where you are
ahead in terms of products or markets, then list
any strengths that have been brought to your
attention while analyzing your customers. Finally,
list the capabilities revealed by
your internal review. To qualify
as a true advantage, a strength
must be recognized as such by
the customer. For example, your
staff may be highly qualified
and motivated, but they can
only be considered a strength if
they provide your customers
with a fast and efficient service.

◀ **SEEKING OPINIONS**
*Meet with customers or suppliers
and ask them for their views on where
you have the advantage over the
competition. They will have an objective
opinion and may well offer interesting
suggestions or insights.*

SUMMARIZING COMPETITIVE ANALYSIS

Examine your analysis of the competition. If your performance is no better than that of your rival, ask yourself why your customers have not switched to another supplier. The answer will reveal your true source of advantage. Alternatively, if your team supplies internal customers, imagine that a new manager has challenged you to justify your existence. The statement of competitive advantage should help you to understand how to win against the competition.

QUESTIONS TO ASK YOURSELF

Q Is our statement of competitive advantage useful in determining which products and services we should sell?

Q Does each advantage put us ahead of all our competitors?

Q Would our main customers agree with the statement?

Q Do our brochures reflect the same advantage?

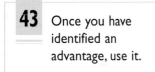

43 Once you have identified an advantage, use it.

▼ **USING YOUR ANALYSIS**
A systematic review of your analysis will enable you to agree on lots of advantages. It is up to you to then decide which ones you are really going to depend upon.

DETERMINING ENDURING ADVANTAGES

There is little point in the team agreeing on a source of advantage that will be lost in the near future. Any advantage should have the potential for surviving at least into year two of the plan. One reason why it is extremely dangerous for organizations to rely on slogans such as "our people are our main source of advantage" is that it makes the organization vulnerable; employees will not stay in the same job forever. Finally, make sure that you express your competitive advantages in terms familiar to your customers to show that they offer real value to them.

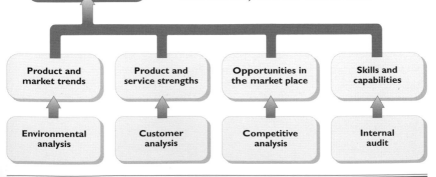

Enduring competitive advantages

Product and market trends — Environmental analysis

Product and service strengths — Customer analysis

Opportunities in the market place — Competitive analysis

Skills and capabilities — Internal audit

SETTING BOUNDARIES

Your customers and prospects will make many demands. You cannot fulfil them all. Draw up definite parameters so that the team is clear about what it will and will not focus on, and ensure that everyone agrees to abide by the boundaries set.

44 Planning what *not* to do is as vital as planning what to do.

45 Choose customers who will be there for the long term.

▼ **AGREEING BOUNDARIES**
If team members have pet schemes or products that they are convinced particular customers would love, now is the time to sell those ideas to the rest of the team. However, they must be prepared to accept boundaries, even if their ideas are rejected – or face leaving the team.

IMPROVING EFFECTIVENESS

Setting boundaries is essential to prevent people wasting time and energy chasing opportunities that are not exactly what the customer needs or what the team wants to deliver. Trying to be all things to all people leads to a lack of team focus, thinly spread resources and, ultimately, failure. Clarifying boundaries early on will help to restrict the choices to be considered later in the planning process. It will also improve operational effectiveness by concentrating on those points that the team believes to be important.

Scheme is rejected, since it oversteps boundaries

Manager notes team member is unhappy

Team member's pet scheme comes up for consideration at team meeting

TARGETING MARKETS AND CUSTOMERS

Rejecting markets and customers is difficult, but understanding the boundaries is vital here, too. It is far better to identify and target customer groups than adopt a "shotgun" approach where any expression of interest is investigated. Draw up a list of what you are going to sell to whom, and what you will not sell. A commercial organization will often target people who pay the best price and give the highest profit margin. An internal organization may focus on customers in the fastest developing part of the business. Make sure the decision on markets is good for the long term.

After discussion, team member agrees to accept decision and keep to boundaries

Manager fails to gain full support of team member

Team member elects to leave the team because he cannot accept boundaries

DRAWING UP BOUNDARIES

Refer to your analysis for guidance

Decide what you are going to sell

Identify who you are going to sell to

Decide what you are not going to sell

Agree who you will not sell to

Write down boundaries and abide by them

46 Make it clear that exceptions to the boundaries set are not allowed.

CHOOSING STRATEGIC EMPHASIS

Your strategic emphasis dictates where you should allocate time and resources. To get the priorities right, look at your products, services, markets, and customers in terms of groups. Bear in mind that circumstances change, so review your emphasis regularly.

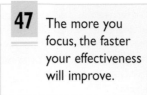

47 The more you focus, the faster your effectiveness will improve.

48 Talk to your suppliers to check that you have grouped products correctly.

GROUPING PRODUCTS AND SERVICES

If you have many different products and services, you will find them far more manageable if you consider them in terms of groups when deciding which are most important. Group products by whatever criteria is appropriate, such as by their complexity. A simple group might require little after-sales support, a complex one might need a lot of support, for example. Or you could group products according to value, size, maturity, or manufacturing process. Exploring creative options for groups can often spark new ideas.

SEGMENTING MARKETS AND CUSTOMERS

Markets and customers can be grouped too, allowing you to focus clearly on a shorter, more specific list. Bear in mind that a more creative approach may reap benefits. The first bank to set up a telephone banking service realized that there was a new group of people to cater to during a strategic planning session. These people wanted to bank using technology rather than visit branches, and to bank outside normal business hours.

POINTS TO REMEMBER

- The more your team focuses its energy and resources, the more effectively it will perform.
- Concentrating on a specific market will make you more knowledgable about your customers' business
- Markets and customers could be segmented by region, size, growth potential, value, or selling process or channel.

ESTABLISHING PRIORITIES

In order to identify which groups are important for today's cash flow and which are going to be important for the long term, examine potential volumes and sales values over the next two to three years. In terms of market forecasts, look at each group in the same way and estimate their current and future sales revenues and/or profits. Consider what each group needs in order to be successful. For example, you may find that one group of products may need automatic packing, while another requires extremely quick distribution. Decide what you have to do to be successful with each product and market group and remember to use this information when you look for gaps in your capabilities later.

49 Encourage debate on priorities to help focus the team.

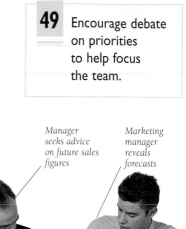

Manager seeks advice on future sales figures

Marketing manager reveals forecasts

FORECASTING SALES ▶
Accurate forecasts of sales volume and value will help you to decide which are the most important areas for emphasis. Ask a colleague from the marketing department for an expert view.

CASE STUDY

Having agreed with her team to choose a new area of emphasis, Jane, the manager, was aware that one of her team members, Derek, was not entirely happy. The change meant that he would be selling to retailers rather than to the distribution customers with whom he had been working for a while. When his performance began to suffer, Jane called Derek into her office at a time when she knew they would not be interrupted and asked for his concerns. He admitted that he felt he knew very little about the retail business and was not confident about his ability to improve sales. Jane was then able to send him on a familiarization course. She also organized a good customer to spend time with Derek explaining the details of retailing. Derek soon got his confidence back, and his sales figures improved dramatically.

◀ ADAPTING TO NEW EMPHASIS
A shift of emphasis can often lead to changes in the way that team members work. In this case, Jane acted promptly when she realized that Derek was having problems in his new area. By arranging extra training and help, she was able to give him confidence and he adapted well to his new area of responsibility.

50 Be realistic; remember that resources for new areas must come from somewhere.

AGREEING EMPHASIS

If the team is to work together to improve overall performance, each member must agree where the strategic emphasis should lie. A split in focus can cause conflict and adversely affect performance, particularly when team members come from different areas of the organization. For example, people who deal with customers may believe that the focus should be on easy-to-sell products, while those responsible for manufacturing more complex products completely disagree. Check that your stakeholders agree with the areas you have chosen to emphasize, too. Use a simple matrix to encourage the team to think about the importance of each product and market. This will help you to agree on the amount of time and resources you are going to put into them in the future.

CULTURAL DIFFERENCES

Nobody doubts the wisdom of trying out markets on a pilot basis. The North Americans tend to be more adventurous in tackling high-volume sales, since their domestic market is so huge. They are less likely than their European colleagues to "wait and see" and risk rival organizations taking the opportunity from them. Asians like to be sure that the market is there before they hit it hard with quality, quantity, and competitive pricing.

▼ DOCUMENTING
CHANGES IN EMPHASIS
Devise a product-market matrix showing where you plan to upgrade and reduce emphasis on products or services. The team can then use this for easy reference.

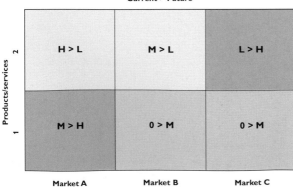

Current > Future

Key

H *High level of activity, that is, occupying many staff and other resources*

M *Medium level of activity*

L *Low level of activity*

0 *No activity at all*

> *Change of emphasis from now to the future*

CHANGING EMPHASIS

As you change products or there are changes to your markets, you will have to change emphasis in each product-market segment as a result. If your customer group is putting such an emphasis on low cost that your profit margin is being badly squeezed, you may choose to downgrade your effort and, over time, withdraw from that segment. How often you do this depends on the volatility of your product markets. Change is particularly rapid in the technology industry, for example, so a software developer may have to review its emphasis on product markets at least twice a year. In the steel industry, on the other hand, emphasis would probably need reviewing only occasionally.

REVIEWING EMPHASIS ▶
It is very easy to become complacent when all is going according to plan. Encourage team members to keep asking questions to make sure that the strategic emphasis is absolutely correct.

QUESTIONS TO ASK YOURSELF

Q Why are we getting such poor sales results from this product market?

Q Are we sure that this product market is going to continue at this growth for another two years?

Q If sales in this area take so much effort, is it worth it?

51 Use logic rather than emotion to find focus.

52 Discuss and agree emphasis with everyone involved.

RESOLVING PROBLEMS

As circumstances change and you review your emphasis, you are likely to notice anomalies and discover areas that no longer deserve so many resources and as much time. Plan to reduce the amount of effort in declining areas and take resources away before the sales value becomes insufficient to pay for the people involved. If you find an area of good potential, now is the time to put in more resources and achieve competitive advantage. Communicating the product-market matrix throughout the company could greatly contribute to getting a cross-functional "one team" view of the whole or part of the organization.

ESTIMATING A BUDGET

Understanding the financial implications of a strategy is fundamental to its success. Look at potential sales volumes, take into account your areas of strategic emphasis, and estimate future costs to arrive at an overall budget.

53 Understand your plan's financial implications to improve its quality.

54 Check that your customer would agree with your sales forecast.

55 Base your budget on realistic sales estimates.

FORECASTING REVENUES

It is important to forecast sales in detail for the next year and at least in outline for two years after that. This is a difficult exercise, but if you miss it out or do it without thought, you risk producing an unrealistic plan; either you will not achieve the sales to make the budget work or you will not be able to supply the number of orders received. Think through your likely sales in terms of optimistic, most likely, and pessimistic, for each product market. In the end, the forecast of what you are committed to sell drives all the other budgets, such as production and distribution.

BECOMING NUMERATE

Accounting is not a natural talent for most people, but in order to plan and follow through strategy successfully, it is important to understand the basics of budgeting and forecasting. If there is any financial issue you do not fully understand, take steps to improve your knowledge, either by reading up

on the subject or by taking an accountancy course. Once you understand the principles of accounting, you will learn from the experience of actually drawing up budgets, writing business plans, doing management accounts, and studying financial reports. This may be a rather laborious process at first, but as you grow increasingly comfortable with managing figures, you will become faster and more skilled at all aspects of accounting.

ESTIMATING COSTS

From your sales forecasts and understanding of your customers' needs, you can make an estimate of any costs involved. Generally, it is useful to break down costs into five categories: people, supplies, facilities, equipment, and information. You may need the help of other stakeholders to complete this stage. For example, it may be useful to know what the IT department intends charging you for information services over the next two to three years. Concentrate on getting numbers that are realistic rather than wholly accurate.

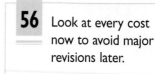

56 Look at every cost now to avoid major revisions later.

▼ **SETTING OUT BUDGETS**
The items of expenditure on this concise budget form have been broken down into five separate categories. The total expenditure and income are then given, followed by the estimated profit.

Budget

The cost of supply of products or anything bought in

The charge that the organization makes for space and other facilities

The total of forecast revenue

Expenditure	Year 1	Year 2	Year 3
People	33,500	36,850	40,535
Supplies	22,000	24,200	26,620
Facilities	12,000	13,200	14,520
Equipment	6,500	7,150	7,865
Information	2,500	2,750	3,025
Total expenditure	76,500	84,150	92,565
Total income	102,000	121,000	139,000
Forecast profit	25,500	36,850	46,435

The total cost of the people in the team

The costs of equipment that the team rents or buys

The charges made for administration

57 Always ask yourself what would happen if sales were to fall.

CALCULATING MARGIN

To work out the operating margin, deduct expenditure from income. In most organizations, there is a standard way of doing budgets. In small organizations, the availability of cash is most important, and it is likely that the team will produce a "cashflow", which is a document showing the timing of payments and receipts. In large organizations, a cashflow is necessary for any team operating in an area where the volume of sales is likely to grow or fall away dramatically.

INTEGRATING STRATEGY

When formulating your plan, make sure that it will integrate well into the organization as a whole. Its aims must be consistent with the plans of other departments to avoid internal conflict and confusion in the market place.

 58 Always present one consistent strategy to your customers.

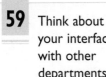 **59** Think about your interfaces with other departments.

 60 Be prepared to give ground in order to reach agreement.

IDENTIFYING POTENTIAL CONFLICT

At every stage in the creation of your plan, look for areas of potential conflict that could jeopardize its success. For example, if strategic thinking is not common practice in your organization, you may, unintentionally, highlight the outmoded and ineffective methods of working of other teams, so act sensitively. Consider whether other teams will understand the need for the changes that you propose. Be sure of your reasons for change before discussing the plan with other teams. Try to work out a mutually acceptable way ahead, and always be prepared to compromise as you move along.

MAKING PROCESSES COMPATIBLE

Always develop your plan with the rest of the organization in mind. If you cannot initiate a new process while an old process remains in place for other teams, determine how this situation can be rectified. Open negotiations with other teams and stimulate thoughts of change and improvement. As team manager, discuss matters with your peers to make the planning process a cycle, so that if one team formulates a plan, the changes required to another team's plan will be anticipated and easy to initiate. As a result, both plans will be improved.

 61 Focus people on the positive aspects of change.

 62 Organize informal discussions on strategy with other teams.

ALIGNING STRATEGIES

The whole process of aligning strategies is made easier where teams follow an agreed procedure, as well as standard techniques and documents, when creating their plans. If your organization does not currently standardize the formulation of its strategic plans, you could always suggest a simple, step-by-step approach. Computer software, for example, has a vital role to play in standardizing procedures, allowing organizations to communicate and update their planning process on line. Stress the benefits to your organization of all teams being able to learn from each other's experiences, as well as from their own.

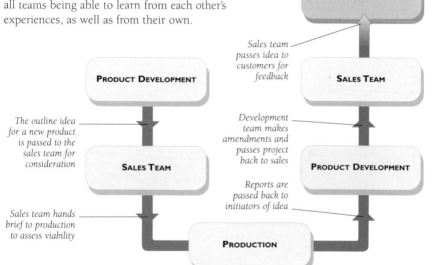

Sales team passes idea to customers for feedback

The outline idea for a new product is passed to the sales team for consideration

Development team makes amendments and passes project back to sales

Reports are passed back to initiators of idea

Sales team hands brief to production to assess viability

CUSTOMER

SALES TEAM

PRODUCT DEVELOPMENT

SALES TEAM

PRODUCT DEVELOPMENT

PRODUCTION

▲ **USING PROCESS MAPS**
When projects involve different teams, use a process map to identify where each stage of a process moves between them. The danger points lie at the handover stage, where delays or misunderstandings may occur. To avoid problems, ensure that each team sees its own part in the process in the context of everyone else's.

63 Many people in your organization have knowledge and experience – make use of these resources.

Testing the Strategy

You now have a strategic plan to which everyone should be committed, until events require you to review and amend it. To maintain the plan's effectiveness, it is important to be able to test current activities and new ideas for strategic fit.

64 Ensure that everyone knows the key tests for a new idea.

65 Keep referring people back to the strategy to maintain focus.

Building a Business Case Template

A business case template enables you to assess whether new ideas fit with your strategy. To create the template, list the most important criteria of your strategy. One criteria, for example, might be to maximize short-term sales. Give each criteria a rating out of 10 that reflects its importance, with 10 being the highest priority. To test a new idea, define how you would ideally meet each criteria. For example, if a criteria is to keep staff to a minimum, you might define the ideal as a reduction in staff. Rate the new idea out of 10 according to how close it comes to the ideal, then multiply the two scores to give a weighting. Ideally, the new idea should score 10 against each criteria, so calculate this. Add up each set of scores to give you total ideal and actual weightings, then work out a percentage.

▼ **TESTING A NEW IDEA**
In the template below, a new idea is measured against three criteria. It scores well against the first and third criteria but not so well against the second. Added together, the weighting scores give a total figure that is translated into a percentage. With 61 per cent, this idea has a reasonable strategic fit.

Criteria (main criteria of strategy)	Priority rating (score 1–10)	New idea (score 1–10)	Weighting (multiply scores)	Ideal weighting (priority x 10)
Increase short-term sales	7	7	49	70
Protect long-term sales	5	2	10	50
Keep staff to minimum	7	8	56	70
Total scores			**115**	**190**
% of ideal				**61%**

To calculate percentage, multiply total weighting score by 100 and divide by total ideal weighting score. The figure reveals how well the idea fits with strategy

USING BUSINESS CASES

It is no good having a well-defined strategy on what you are going to sell and to whom if, in reality, everyone ignores it. Encourage the team to use the business case as a matter of course, both to check what they are doing currently (are they concentrating on the agreed strategic emphasis?) and to test every new opportunity for viability. Adopting such a logical process for assessing current and new plans encourages team members to view issues objectively. The more the business case template is used, the more experienced the team will become at evaluating suggestions. Additionally, once team members realize exactly what the criteria and ideal are, they will be more likely to make suggestions that come close to these important requirements.

66 Make it clear that all new ideas must be tested against the template.

67 Look at the risk of ideas not going as well as hoped.

◀ CLARIFYING THE PROCESS
Make sure that the team understands how new opportunities will be evaluated. Having a formal process for reviewing ideas emphasizes that all suggestions are important and will be taken seriously.

CASE STUDY

Peter, a sales executive for a frozen foods firm, had the idea of offering a new home delivery service to domestic clients. A survey of customers revealed that many would welcome the service. He decided to test his idea against the business case template to see whether it fitted the company strategy. The template had three criteria: short-term sales had a high priority; quality of service medium priority; and

long-term sales high priority. He had a high score against the first criteria but needed to score highly against the third, too. In a trade newspaper, Peter found results of a national survey showing that home delivery, with orders coming from the Internet as well as the telephone, were set to grow hugely. This meant that his proposal scored well against the template, and a project to start home delivery was put into place.

◀ USING A BUSINESS CASE
Peter's boss had made him fully aware that any new ideas for the company should be tested against the business case template. This meant that Peter could take it upon himself to come up with a well-argued and easy-to-implement idea. He knew that the idea would work with the overall strategy because he had been able to test its viability himself.

COMMUNICATING CLEARLY

For your strategy to succeed, it is vital that everyone who needs to know about it is informed. Communicate your plan to every stakeholder so that they understand what the strategy will do for them, and you will gain their commitment to it.

 68 If people do not know what you are trying to do, they cannot help.

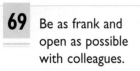 **69** Be as frank and open as possible with colleagues.

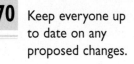 **70** Keep everyone up to date on any proposed changes.

KEEPING STAKEHOLDERS INFORMED

Since stakeholders – whether superiors, colleagues in other departments, team members who have not been involved in the entire planning process, or customers and suppliers – have a vested interest in the strategic plan, each of them needs to be kept informed of developments relevant to them. Keep the language you use simple and define all important terms; even a word such as "sale" can have different meanings to different people within the same organization.

GETTING FEEDBACK

Whichever method of communication you use, make sure that there is a feedback mechanism in place whereby stakeholders can let you know what they think of the plan and its impact on them. Everyone in the organization should be viewed as the eyes and ears of the team. The salespeople, for example, know what the customers are saying, just as site engineers will have an insider's view of how work is progressing. Each has a role to play in checking and moulding the final version of the strategy. So make sure communication is two-way and listen. Then listen some more. Use feedback in a review meeting to spark changes and improvements to the plan.

CULTURAL DIFFERENCES

In the UK and, to a certain extent, Scandinavia, metaphors, similes, and irony are used extensively in business dealings, not to be impolite but to strongly emphasize a point. In the US, Canada, and Germany, such figures of speech are more likely to be taken literally, causing possible, unintended offence.

COMMUNICATING THE STRATEGY

METHOD OF COMMUNICATION	FACTORS TO CONSIDER

DETAILED REPORT
The whole plan, including the planning process and change projects.

- Documentation should be clearly laid out and backed up with the analysis information.
- Only superiors and key team members should receive the plan in its entirety.

OUTLINE REPORT
A one-page outline of the strategy; extracts of the plan relevant to the stakeholder.

- This report should be personalized for stakeholders, stressing factors that will have a direct effect on them.
- Any other parties who might benefit from the information can receive an outline report.

PRESENTATION
A summary of the strategy and implementation plan using visual aids.

- Presentation material must look professional and convincing.
- Team members, internal stakeholders, and manager's peer group should be invited.

NEWSLETTERS
Updates on the progress of the strategy and plan.

- Reports should be kept brief and circulated to team members and stakeholders regularly.
- Preparing newsletters can be delegated to a key team member.

LETTERS AND E-MAILS
Specific extracts from the strategy and plan, or updates on change projects.

- These are quick to produce and useful for keeping a large number of people updated.
- Stakeholders with a limited interest in the strategy need only minimal information.

GAINING COMMITMENT

When communicating the strategy, encourage your audience to ask themselves the question, "So what does this mean to me and the way I do my job?" This helps them to understand the strategy. Ask people to commit to their role in the plan, and, where it is important, confirm those commitments in writing. Communicating the plan is also a continuous process. Ensure you keep those who need to know regularly updated on progress.

71 Aim to finish off communications with a summary of agreed actions.

IMPLEMENTING A STRATEGY

Implementing a strategic plan involves setting change projects in motion that will achieve strategic aims. Learn how to change for the future while maximizing performance today.

PRIORITIZING CHANGE

The first step in implementing a strategy is to identify areas for improvement. Compare the current situation with the ideal to see where there are gaps, then group changes that are critical to your strategy into areas for immediate action.

72 Learn to live with business processes that you are unable to change.

73 Always aim for the best possible result.

74 Deal with the most important areas for improvement first.

LISTING IMPROVEMENTS

Draw up a comprehensive list of between 50 to 100 issues that need improvement in order for the new strategy to succeed. This will provide you with the starting point for planning the changes. You can compile this list yourself if it comes easily to you, or you can ask key members of the team to brainstorm it with you. Pose the question, "Given what we are trying to achieve, how, in an ideal world, would our organization operate in the areas of business processes, technology, and people?" This will lead to several answers. You now know what would be ideal.

IDENTIFYING GAPS

By reviewing your current situation and comparing it to the ideal, you will reveal gaps. These will probably never be fully closed, since there is always room for improvements. Nevertheless the major gaps – the ones you must do something about – will be clear. At the opposite end of the scale, there will be much less important gaps where improvements would be desirable but not necessarily essential.

SETTING PRIORITIES

List each area for improvement and mark it as high, medium, or low under the categories of impact and urgency. You have no option but to deal with those changes that have a high impact and high urgency. Use the measure to prioritize the changes, then group them so that you arrive at, say, eight to 10 areas for change. These groupings are called "change projects". As you implement your strategy, the team should find itself tackling high-impact changes before they become high-urgency.

THINGS TO DO

1. Look at your processes, such as how you handle customer orders.
2. Assess whether you need to upgrade your technology.
3. Look at staffing structure: might smaller teams serve the customer better?
4. Check that you have the right people with the necessary skills on the team.
5. Look at support resources: does the team have back-up?

▼ COMPARING PRIORITIES

The good prioritizing team looks ahead and tackles critical jobs first, giving them control over the strategy. Bad prioritizers react to the past and put off demanding activities, leading to loss of control.

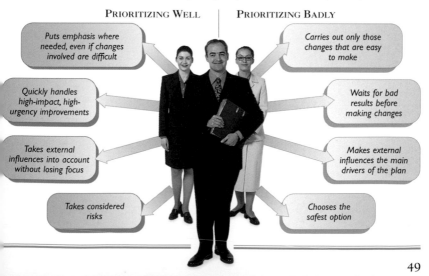

PRIORITIZING WELL | PRIORITIZING BADLY

Puts emphasis where needed, even if changes involved are difficult

Carries out only those changes that are easy to make

Quickly handles high-impact, high-urgency improvements

Waits for bad results before making changes

Takes external influences into account without losing focus

Makes external influences the main drivers of the plan

Takes considered risks

Chooses the safest option

PLANNING CHANGE

Bringing about effective change is vital to strategic success. Take a disciplined approach and work out action plans for all your change projects with objectives, milestones, and time-scales. These then form part of your overall implementation plan.

75 If change will not bring definite benefits, it is not worthwhile.

MOVING FORWARD

76 Look for big improvements from change projects.

Change projects are aimed at improving long-term operational effectiveness and could take from a few weeks to two years or more to complete, depending on the complexity and degree of change involved. Break down each project into an action plan, with estimated start and end dates. As you change for the future, continue with operational plans and targets that rule how you run today's business. Once change projects are under way, you may then need to review operations to accommodate them.

LEARNING FROM THE PAST

Keep good notes as you tackle each change project, so that you or your colleagues can refer to them in the future when similar challenges present themselves. Find out whether anyone in the organization has had experience of making the same type of changes that you are planning and ask to borrow their notes. Referring to what has been done before may give you valuable insights into the task at hand.

KEEPING A RECORD ▶
Update progress notes regularly so that you can make them immediately available to colleagues who may need to carry out similar activities urgently.

77 When wording objectives, make them unambiguous.

POINTS TO REMEMBER

- The wording of the objective should be clear enough to enable people who are new to the team to understand it.
- Each change project may have several objectives.
- Most people prefer a set objective to a list of tasks because it provides more of a challenge.

DEFINING OBJECTIVES

Before deciding on an action plan, make sure you have defined exactly what each change project is trying to achieve and by when. It is important to produce objectives that are as tight and specific as possible. Follow the SMART rule, a useful management acronym that defines objectives as:

- Stretching – they should challenge the manager and the team;
- Measurable – they must be quantifiable;
- Achievable – they must be realistic;
- Related to the customer – they should improve service to them;
- Time-targeted – they must have be an end date.

By setting such objectives you ensure that everyone has a clear definition of what you hope to gain and a better understanding of the value of the change.

ALLOCATING RESPONSIBILITY

Change projects can be tricky to implement since many people are resistant to change. A major change in attitude, such as changing your customers' perception of your company, can also be a long and difficult process. Yet for the change to happen, someone must take overall responsibility for it. Usually, the team member with the most relevant experience takes charge. If it is not obvious who this should be, then it falls to the manager.

Team member takes ownership of the project

Colleague agrees to assist but does not take responsibility

TAKING ▶ RESPONSIBLITY

Each change project should be overseen by a single team member who is held accountable. The person responsible then has the task of making sure that everyone else in the team does what is required.

SETTING MILESTONES

Change projects, by their nature, are often far-reaching. If, for example, you are trying to redefine all your business processes, you will not be able to succeed overnight. Having established the objective of the change project, it is important to set some milestones as steps on the way to success so that the team can check if the change project is on track. Ask yourself, "What do I need to do to reach each milestone?", and break down the work into a series of tasks. Milestones may be events, such as producing a report, or they may be achievements – for example, getting the agreement of a director to allocate resources to review the sales order processing system.

THINGS TO DO

1. Set out milestones that allow you to measure progress periodically.

2. Draw up clear and unambiguous directives that everyone will understand.

3. Keep stakeholders up to date with progress and any changes to the plan.

4. Check that team members feel confident of achieving their milestones.

74 Make sure the team's priorities are the same as yours.

SETTING TIME TARGETS

Achieving change takes time. However, if the change is urgent but the problem has little short-term impact, there is a danger that the team will put a low priority on their part in the change project. By setting time targets you make sure that people are not sidetracked by operational issues. Emphasize to the team that failure to change now will seriously hurt performance in the future. If you have effectively specified accountability and set a time-scale, you will be able to answer the question, "If this change does not occur by this date, whom do we hold responsible?"

◀ AGREEING TIME-SCALES
Make sure that time targets are demanding but achievable. It is a good idea to discuss targets with team members to ensure they are realistic and stress that you expect them to be met.

Recording Progress

Each change project action plan should be updated regularly and made available to any team member who needs it. Put all the plans, together with all the necessary back-up documents available, into one large folder, as a record of all aspects of the implementation of your strategic plan. You should also include the research carried out during the analysis. You may also wish to store all the information in an electronic file, to which all members have access. Keep the data practical. Refer back to the folder or electronic file yourself and encourage the team to do so to keep the document dynamic and in use from day to day.

▼ DOCUMENTING CHANGE PROJECTS

Teams must take change projects as seriously as they take a project involved in delivering products to a customer. Use the discipline of clear documentation.

75 Remember that an action plan is not complete until it is written down.

A clear, SMART statement of the project objective

The deadlines by which the changes needs to be made

An event or achievement marking the progress of a change project

Key events that allow you to monitor if the project is on track to finish in time

CHANGE PROJECT ACTION PLAN

Objective To implement a new sales ordering processing system within a budget of £50,000	
Measure A reduction in our debt collection days from 80 days on average to 50 days on average	
Deadline Pilot by end January next year, and full implementation by September	**Owner** RHC
Actions Agree the attributes of the new system with internal departments and customers	**Time** March 28
	Responsibility ASD
Milestones Recommendation agreed by Board	**Time** June 11
	Responsibility RHC

The qualification by which the objectives may be measured

The person with overall responsibility for achieving objective

Date by which action should be completed

Person responsible for the action

ASSESSING THE RISKS

Having tested the strategy for problems during the planning stage, now review the change project plans to ascertain what might prevent them from succeeding. List potential threats and, if necessary, alter the plans to minimize them.

80 Always rehearse a contingency plan to make it more useful.

81 Ask stakeholders what they think could go wrong.

82 Greet the unexpected as an opportunity rather than a threat.

PREDICTING PROBLEMS

Bring the team together with the sole purpose of brainstorming a list of possible future problems. Look at each action plan in turn and ask the question, "What could prevent this from happening?" This process encourages the team to defend the plan against constructive criticism, with the result that they will be even more confident in working within the strategy and more committed to overcoming any future obstacles. Avoid listing every potential problem but concentrate instead on those that have at least a 50 per cent chance of actually occurring.

ASSESSING IMPACT

Since potential problems will vary in importance, look at the likely impact of each problem, and ask the team to assess whether such problems could prevent the change project from being completed on time. Consider whether the impact of each problem on the project will be high, medium, or low. Assess the probability that each threat will occur. Mark these high, medium, or low. As your [te]am members implement the strategy and begin [to] think long term, they will inevitably spend [mo]re time on high-probability but low-impact [even]ts. When this occurs, they will be in better [contr]ol of their business environment and strategy.

POINTS TO REMEMBER

- People should be encouraged to treat problems as another challenge of change.
- By changing the plan, it might be possible to completely avoid a potential problem without impacting the strategy.
- It is important not only to look at the current situation when assessing problems but also at two to three years further on.
- A change of customer or supplier could pose a significant threat to success.

AVOIDING TROUBLE

The most significant threats are those with the potential for the greatest impact and with the highest probability of occurrence. Change or add to an action plan to prevent them. For example, another stakeholder may be able to mitigate a certain threat. Approach them to find out whether the problem can be avoided, or whether the milestone or objective under threat is not feasible. If the latter is the case, you will have to think again.

Stakeholder envisages what could go wrong

Team member explains a change in procedure

SEEKING NEW INSIGHTS ▶

It is important to talk to stakeholders, either in the normal course of events or in a special meeting, about how change projects will affect them. The stakeholders may provide valuable new insights into potential problems.

PRE-EMPTING TROUBLE ▼

By taking early action, Laura ensured that software delivery was delayed for less than a month, customer service was maintained, and problems caused by the delayed completion date were minimized.

CONTINGENCY PLANNING

You will not be able to pre-empt all significant problems, but you can certainly think through alternative ways of achieving the milestones or objectives under threat. This is called contingency planning, and it ensures that the team reacts smoothly and quickly should a predicted potential problem occur. Sometimes you may just have to wait to see if a problem arises, and then respond, but if you have assessed the risks well, you will be far better prepared to react sv and effectively. It sense to install sprinkler sy there is a

CASE STUDY

Laura ran a computer help desk for her head office. She and her team planned a major change project to improve the computer system and provide a better service to customers. A vital piece of software they needed for this was in the final stages of testing, and Laura knew that if the software was supplied late, they would be unable to switch over to the new system on time, or even maintain their current level of service. It was, in Laura's opinion, a high-impact, high-probability risk. She talked to her supplier who agreed that if the software was not delivered on time, he would lend her two staff until it was. They also agreed that Laura would pay their salaries for the first month but that the supplier would pay them thereafter. The team then warned its customers about the potential delay to the new system and explained the contingency plan.

REVIEWING OPERATIONAL TARGETS

A new strategy will almost certainly mean changes to operational targets. Agree new targets collectively for the team, and individually for each team member; then, as targets are achieved, look for ways of making further improvements.

 83 Treat people as if they want to succeed, and they will do their best.

 84 Set targets that will help to develop the team.

 85 Allow people to decide how to meet their targets.

SETTING NEW TARGETS

Translate the top-level objectives of the plan into specific measurable targets at the next level, and so on down the team. For example, when a sales team agrees to a strategy it may well agree on what market share the team is trying to achieve. This is then broken down into individual sales targets which, if all are hit, will achieve the overall target for market share. Performance targets, even when there are only two levels, are part of a hierarchy where top-level performance is delivered through achieving targets spread around the organization.

ENSURING REALISTIC TARGETS

Make targets stretching but achievable. If you set a target that carries little challenge, you will not get the best from people. If you set a target that is virtually impossible, either they will not try or they will come under too much pressure. As manager, it is a good time to make people enthusiastic about the new opportunities and challenges ahead. Make sure team members committed to their new targets and feel good about their ability to achieve them.

POINTS TO REMEMBER

- If everyone hits their targets and most people over-achieve significantly, the targets were probably too low.
- It is better for people to succeed on a realistic target than, for the same performance, to fail on an over-ambitious one.
- The sum of the team's targets should be greater than the overall target set, in order to allow for any shortfalls.

86 Explain to the team how strategic thinking will benefit performance today as well as tomorrow.

MAKING IMPROVEMENTS

As the team achieves new targets, the strategy will develop and you will be able to look for further progress and improvement. Most organizations compete in markets where customer expectations are increasing regularly and competitors are getting better at satisfying them. Ensure that your internal targets keep in step with this. You may have brought costs down below last year, but can you keep them at that level and improve on quality? Do not wait for the start of a new company year to discuss targets. Review them continuously and encourage people to want to be more productive.

Superior agrees to put in more resources in the expectation of better results

Manager explains how a new opportunity will enable her to achieve higher targets

IMPROVING OPERATIONAL PERFORMANCE

Implement a new strategy

Carry out change projects

Review operational targets

Produce a team operating plan

Create individual operating plans

Achieve improved results

◀ USING TARGETS TO WIN BACKING

Targets can be used as bargaining tools. If you need more resources to exploit an opportunity, you are likely to gain approval if you can meet higher target. and show when, and in what quant. the improved results will com

MOTIVATING PEOPLE

A new strategy brings fresh challenges and opportunities. Motivate everyone involved by ensuring that they appreciate the part they have to play in making it a success. Then encourage the team through training and rewarding their achievements.

87 Always assume that people really want to achieve more.

REVIEWING ROLES AND RESPONSIBILITIES

If a team adopts a new strategy, almost all of its members and other stakeholders will have to change their behaviour and adjust to the new requirements of the job. Take the opportunity to review all roles and responsibilities. Create an attitude that says, "It is no longer enough to turn up to do the job we did yesterday; instead we all have a responsibility to find ways in which we can improve." Hold discussions individually with team members, perhaps at the same time as you discuss new operating targets, to ensure that they are happy with any changes. Then ask appropriate team members to talk to stakeholders. It is important that everyone involved understands their new responsibilities, including managers in your organization, customers, and suppliers.

▲ **INVOLVING CUSTOMERS**

Customers will be far more enthusiastic and cooperative if you make them feel volved. Appoint a key team member to lain the strategy and the reasons for changes, and ask customers to confirm agreement. Get written confirmation hanges proposed are significant.

DO'S AND DON'TS

✔ Do encourage suggestions from the team on ways to change and improve.

✔ Do ensure that team members completely understand their new roles.

✘ Don't allow incentive schemes to reward people for working outside the strategy

✘ Don't imagine that roles set at start of the year will still be appropriate at the end.

88 If raising targets, listen to feedback to improve the chance of success.

89 Set the highest standards, both for yourself and for others.

INVESTING IN TRAINING

By changing roles and responsibilities, you may find that previously well-qualified team members now lack the skills to achieve new targets. What skills will your staff need for future roles? For example, given that technology is changing so rapidly, do they possess the know-how to work with the latest computer software? You will encourage people to implement strategy more effectively if it integrates into their normal business lives, such as by building the use of computers and software into the implementation. Bear in mind that people will not need to master new skills or learn facts that can be provided through technology when required.

REWARDING PEOPLE

Check that the old reward system still fits the new environment. If you have changed targets, roles, and responsibilities, you may have to offer new rewards and incentives. Remember that mentoring and coaching are an essential part of an environment where you are continuously trying to improve service to customers and team performance. Give your team the support it needs to do the new job well, and help stakeholders to play their roles as fully as possible. Recognition and feedback are as important as financial rewards. Give people feedback when they get it right as well as when they get it wrong. Is anyone on your team likely to say, "I do not know whether or not I am doing a good job"? If the answer is yes, you still have some work to do to agree targets, roles, responsibilities, and rewards.

▼ **SAYING THANK YOU**
One of the easiest and most effective forms of reward is to say thank you for a job well done. Praising an individual in front of fellow team members reinforces the message and inspires confidence.

MONITORING PERFORMANCE

To keep the plan on track, closely monitor progress in both operational plans and change projects. Organize team reports that signal shortfalls or problems to be corrected, and look at progress across the organization where it impacts your plans.

90 Give people only the level of detail they really need.

▲ **INDICATING PROBLEMS**
Use a green, red, and amber "traffic light" system to monitor progress. Amber or red indicators denote issues that must be tackled at the next review meeting.

ORGANIZING REPORTS

Performance reports must show what progress has been made to date towards the targets set. A useful technique is to use red, amber and green indicators to chart progress. For example, if you are half-way through a year in which the target is to produce 1,000 units, and you have made about 500, the status of this target is "green". If production problems have led to only 380 units being made, the status of this target should be recorded as "amber", and the item should be discussed at the next review meeting. If you have only produced 150 units, the status indicator will be set at "red". This signals that urgent action is required or that the target has become impossible to achieve.

MONITORING CHANGE PROJECTS

You can also use green, red, and amber status indicators to monitor change projects. If most milestones are being achieved, the status should be green. If there are problems, it is the responsibility of the manager or the team member in charge of the project to alert the team that the status has changed to amber. If there are serious problems, the team must be informed of the red status immediately, and a course of action must be proposed to remedy the situation.

ASSESSING THE PROGRESS OF OTHERS

In addition to producing your own reports, it is important to keep a close check on the performance of people outside your team if their progress is likely to affect your targets or change projects. If, for example, production is falling behind on a new range of goods and you are a sales manager with a target of selling a specific number of units, you will need to know of any shortfall. Try to persuade people in other departments to use the same standard methods of producing reports, since this will make understanding them far easier. To make certain that the information contained in a report is timely and accurate, someone must also be responsible for it. Allocate this task to a team member who is responsible for some of the items in the report itself. Stress the importance of keeping reports clear and up-to-date – and hope that others will follow your good example.

91 Monitor informally by listening, observing, and communicating.

92 Keep up to date with changes in other areas of your organization.

▼ **MONITORING EFFECTIVELY**
The diagram below shows how important it is to have a monitoring system that warns of the gap between target and progress before it becomes critical. After that point, it may be impossible to get a change project back on track. Operational targets may need monitoring weekly rather than monthly.

Problem is recognized at monthly meeting

Action is taken to resolve problem

Problem is recognized but too late to save project

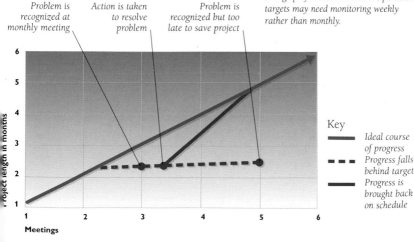

Project length in months

Meetings

Key

— Ideal course of progress

- - - Progress falls behind target

— Progress is brought back on schedule

HOLDING REVIEWS

M onthly review meetings allow you to examine the operational issues of the day and resolve any problems highlighted by progress reports. It is also important to set aside time to look at the overall strategy and ensure that it is still relevant.

93 Be firm when running meetings; keep them strictly to the point.

94 Make it a hard and fast rule to start and finish meetings on time.

CONDUCTING REVIEWS ▼
Address urgent issues first, giving each team member the opportunity to come up with solutions. If a solution is not obvious, delegate the problem to the appropriate people to be resolved after the meeting.

REVIEWING PROGRESS

Like a board of directors, teams typically meet once a month. Use the status indicators – red, amber, or green – to establish the order of your agenda. Monitor the operational past by asking how you have done, and consider the likely outcome if you leave things as they are. Look at change projects and assess whether you are actually making changes in the way you intended. Finally, check your assumptions. Is your plan still valid in all aspects? The answers will prompt a number of suggestions for changing how you work.

Team leader begins review by discussing urgent, or "red", item

Team member responsible for change project explains problems

Colleague suggests possible remedial action

Team member agrees to assist in getting objective back on track

RESOLVING ISSUES

Discuss indicators that show that immediate action is required. For example, if there is a delay in delivering products to an important customer, the team must decide what it is going to do about it, agree who is responsible for resolving the issue, and put a time limit on finding a solution. Discussion of progress against change projects is almost always useful, and often the whole team will have a contribution to make. If a point comes up regularly and shows no improvement, check what action is feasible and change the plan rather than leaving the subject to fester.

- If a change project takes place over a long period of time, you need to make sure that it stays fresh in everyone's mind.
- The whole team should be involved in discussing change projects that are developing more slowly than expected.
- It is useful to have a superior present at certain review meetings, particularly if you anticipate having to ask for more resources.

95 If plans are not working, change them now rather than later.

96 Use review meetings to test new ideas against the business case.

REVIEWING STRATEGY

Use monthly meetings to concentrate on operational targets and change projects that are already under way. You should also hold longer meetings on a regular basis to review the strategy itself if your plan is to retain its relevance, and to make sure it is still the best plan the team can devise. Check the assumptions you identified at the fact-gathering stage to confirm they are still the best estimates. It is unlikely that you will need to go back to stating purpose or to examine your competitive advantage or boundary setting at every quarterly meeting, but you may have to regroup product markets, change emphasis on product markets, and have another look at budgets.

DO'S AND DON'TS

✔ Do remind people that completed change projects will ultimately benefit them.

✔ Do expect everyone to carry out their actions in change projects.

✘ Don't accept excuses that everyday pressure is preventing work on change projects.

✘ Don't leave more than one month between reviews.

97 Consider changes to the business case template itself, if necessary.

BEING FLEXIBLE

An army general once said: "No plan survives contact with the enemy." Similarly, it is said that no strategic plan survives contact with the market place. Be prepared to change the plan in the light of new circumstances and the unforeseen.

98 Aim to improve continuously to be flexible strategically.

EXPECTING THE UNEXPECTED

Not all eventualities can be predicted. External events may force you to review a basic part of the plan only a short time into implementation. A radical change, such as a competitor launching a new product or an important customer merging with another company, will have a major impact on the strategy. Whenever this happens, and certainly every year, you must re-examine the plan for its overall statement of direction.

In a review meeting, team spots the need to change the plan

Team postpones review and fails to recognize that change is needed

Team finalizes the strategic plan

Team fails to deliver and customer expresses lack of confidence

▲ ADAPTING TO CHANGE

In this example, a team is faced with external changes in the market. The effective team discusses the changes, decides to change its plan, and informs the customer, boosting his confidence in the team. The team that fails to spot the changes, or ignores them, risks losing its customers.

99 Listen to what suppliers say about changes in their industry.

Customer is impressed by forward-thinking and increases business

ALTERING COURSE

Be prepared to change the strategic plan as and when necessary. In fact, one of the paybacks of developing a good strategic plan is that even in fast-moving business environments, the strategy provides the basis on which to evaluate opportunities. To be effective, you and your team must constantly challenge your current methods of conducting business and seek to change and improve the ways in which you meet customer needs. Review meetings offer an excellent platform for the discussion of these ideas. A difficult situation arises if, for example, a pet project for a new product has been made irrelevant by a competitor offering something radically better. Just as your reviewing system must allow for new opportunities, it must also provide a mechanism for discarding ideas that were originally sound. New opportunities require resources, and it is not unusual for these resources to come from existing activities or projects.

RE-TESTING STRATEGY

The strategy at the end of a planning year may differ significantly from the initial plan, but, provided that the team has applied the agreed criteria for assessing business cases, it will still reflect the best speed and direction of development. The benefit of using the business case template will be seen again when the team makes a change to the strategy. By subjecting a change, such as a new emphasis on a product market, to the business case template test, you will see which opportunities you should exploit. Finally, there will be times when even the business case template may need reviewing. But that is what strategic thinking is all about: keeping up to date and improving all the time.

100 Make sure you react to change with courage and resolution.

101 Remember that strategic thinking should be fun as well as challenging.

ASSESSING YOUR STRATEGIC THINKING

E valuate your ability to think strategically by responding to the following statements, marking the option closest to your experience. Be as honest as you can: if your answer is "never", circle Option 1; if it is "always", circle Option 4, and so on. Add your scores together, and refer to the Analysis to see how well you scored. Use your answers to identify the areas that most need improvement.

OPTIONS
1 Never
2 Occasionally
3 Frequently
4 Always

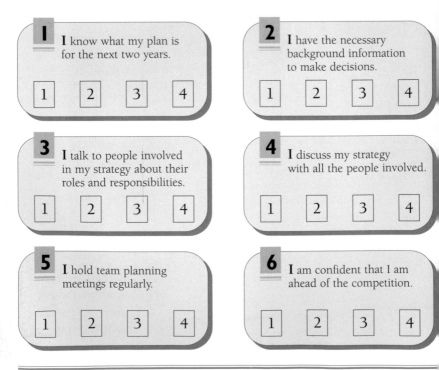

1 I know what my plan is for the next two years.

1   2   3   4

2 I have the necessary background information to make decisions.

1   2   3   4

3 I talk to people involved in my strategy about their roles and responsibilities.

1   2   3   4

4 I discuss my strategy with all the people involved.

1   2   3   4

5 I hold team planning meetings regularly.

1   2   3   4

6 I am confident that I am ahead of the competition.

1   2   3   4

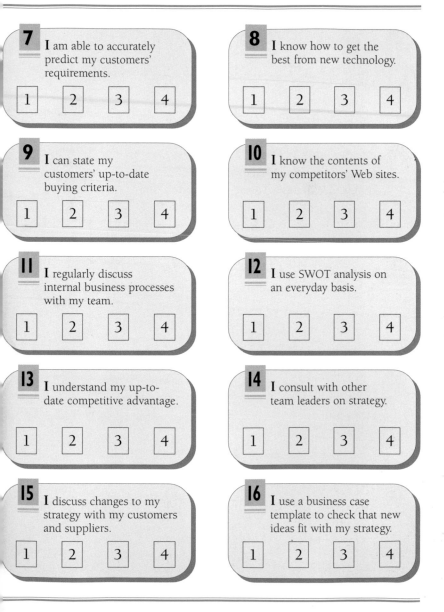

7 I am able to accurately predict my customers' requirements.

1 2 3 4

8 I know how to get the best from new technology.

1 2 3 4

9 I can state my customers' up-to-date buying criteria.

1 2 3 4

10 I know the contents of my competitors' Web sites.

1 2 3 4

11 I regularly discuss internal business processes with my team.

1 2 3 4

12 I use SWOT analysis on an everyday basis.

1 2 3 4

13 I understand my up-to-date competitive advantage.

1 2 3 4

14 I consult with other team leaders on strategy.

1 2 3 4

15 I discuss changes to my strategy with my customers and suppliers.

1 2 3 4

16 I use a business case template to check that new ideas fit with my strategy.

1 2 3 4

17 I ensure that my team members know the criteria for adopting new ideas.

1   2   3   4

18 I ensure that my team always operates within the strategy.

1   2   3   4

19 I have drawn up appropriate priorities for product markets.

1   2   3   4

20 I put resources into new markets with potential but little short-term profit.

1   2   3   4

21 I know what my costs are against budget.

1   2   3   4

22 I know what my actual sales are against target.

1   2   3   4

23 I know exactly where my team needs to improve on its skills.

1   2   3   4

24 I ensure that team members take change projects seriously.

1   2   3   4

25 I have a documented and up-to-date strategic plan.

1   2   3   4

26 I know what the threats are to achieving my objectives.

1   2   3   4

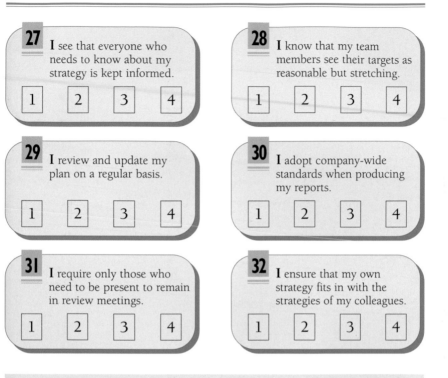

27 I see that everyone who needs to know about my strategy is kept informed.

1   2   3   4

28 I know that my team members see their targets as reasonable but stretching.

1   2   3   4

29 I review and update my plan on a regular basis.

1   2   3   4

30 I adopt company-wide standards when producing my reports.

1   2   3   4

31 I require only those who need to be present to remain in review meetings.

1   2   3   4

32 I ensure that my own strategy fits in with the strategies of my colleagues.

1   2   3   4

ANALYSIS

Now that you have completed the self-assessment, add up your total score and check your performance by reading the corresponding evaluation. Whichever level of success you have achieved in thinking strategically, it is important to remember that there is always room for improvement. Identify your weakest areas, and refer to the relevant section and chapters where you will find practical advice and tips to help you to develop and refine your skills.

32–64: You operate reactively and do not spend enough time thinking strategically. Take one or two individual steps from the planning process and see them through to a result.
65–95: You are a reasonable strategic thinker, but should address some weak points.
96–128: You are a good strategic thinker, but do not become complacent.

INDEX

ACKNOWLEDGMENTS

AUTHORS' ACKNOWLEDGMENTS

An impressive team of skilled people were involved in producing this book. In particular we would like to thank Adèle Hayward and Caroline Marklew of Dorling Kindersley for their help in sorting out the concepts, structure, and overall design of the book. Arthur Brown brought constructive and creative ideas to the detailed design stage, and Amanda Lebentz is the most positive and meticulous editor you could hope to have. We gratefully acknowledge their huge contributions.

PUBLISHER'S ACKNOWLEDGMENTS

Dorling Kindersley would like to thank the following for their help and participation in producing this book:

Photography Matthew Ward.

Models Roger Andre, Anne Chapman, Brent Clark, Emma Harris, Nigel Hill, Gill Hooton, Sander deGroot, Sophie Millett, Roger Mundy, Anastasia Vengeroua, Michael Weinkove.

Make-up Evelynne.

Picture research Andy Sansom.
Picture library assistance Melanie Simmonds.

Indexer Hilary Bird.

PICTURE CREDITS

Key: *a* above, *b* bottom, *c* centre, *l* left, *r* right, *t* top
Colorific M Hardwick 60; **Powerstock** 39; **Telegraph Colour Library** Paul Campbell 17, Ryanstock 32; **Tony Stone Images** Peter Correz, front jacket, Ken Fisher 4, Stephen Peters 11 *tl*.

AUTHORS' BIOGRAPHIES

Andy Bruce is the founder of SofTools Limited – a specialist business research and consulting company. Following completion of a largely academic MBA programme, he has spent the past eight years helping a variety of organizations redefine strategy and cope with change in the real world – more information on tools and techniques can be found at www.SofTools.net.

Ken Langdon has a background in sales and marketing in the computer industry. As an independent consultant he has lectured on strategic thinking and planning in the USA, Europe, and Australasia. He has helped companies, big and small, to review their strategies at board level and widely at team level. Companies for whom he has provided strategic guidance include computer majors such as Hewlett Packard, and utilities companies such as a European electricity supplier.